Raccoons

by K. M. Kostyal

A little raccoon holds on to the trunk of a tree.

BOOKS FOR YOUNG EXPLORERS
NATIONAL GEOGRAPHIC SOCIETY

Did you know that young raccoons play together, the way you and your friends do? These cubs are chasing each other on a dock. Now one is hanging upside down and touching the water with its nose.

Raccoons live in forests and in wet places and in cities. They even live on grasslands and on islands. Are there raccoons living near you?

A young raccoon peeks from a hole in a tree.
The hole makes a safe place for its den,
or home. Raccoons may use a large birdhouse
for a den, too. They are smart, curious animals.
They spend a lot of their time exploring.

In the spring, a mother raccoon has babies. Several fuzzy little cubs, smaller than your hand, are born in the den. Like all baby mammals, they drink their mother's milk.

At first, they just eat and sleep. Their mother takes care of them. Later, they will scamper and play and learn how to take care of themselves.

Very gently, a mother raccoon carries
her cub in her mouth. When the cub is
about two months old, it will begin
following its mother as she explores.

Cubs learn by watching what their
mother does, then copying her.
If she digs in river mud,
looking for food, they will dig, too.

Climbing is an important skill for a raccoon cub to learn. It will spend a lot of its life up in trees.

Sharp claws help the cub hang on tight to tree bark.
With a little practice, the cub will become a good climber.

When a raccoon goes looking for food, it may stop to take a snooze. A tree branch or a hole under rocks is a good place for a nap.

Raccoons have special ways of climbing down trees. Sometimes, they turn their feet almost backward and climb down headfirst.

Big juicy grapes make a good meal for a raccoon. Raccoons eat all kinds of food. They nibble on corn from farmers' fields and on nuts they find in the woods.

In the fall, raccoons eat a lot and grow fat. Food may be hard to find in the winter. This one has caught a little fish for its dinner. It might snack on eggs in a duck's nest, too.

Look at that raccoon's long fingers!
See the reflection in the water.
The paw prints of a raccoon show five
fingers. A raccoon picks things up
with its fingers, as you do.

Raccoons find food with their hands.
This female has felt around in the mud
for a snail. You may see a raccoon
put its food in water. We don't know
just why it does this, but it seems to
like to play with its food.

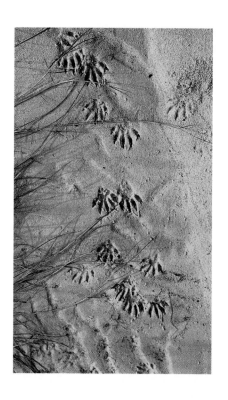

Could you catch a fish with your hands?
A raccoon can. Its hands feel things easily
in water and can quickly grab a fish.

Circling in the snow, a fox and
a raccoon growl at each other.
The raccoon lowers its head and
lifts its back. This makes it look
bigger than it really is.

A snarling cougar cannot quite reach
a raccoon, high up in a tree.
Raccoons are not fast runners,
but they can quickly climb a tree
when enemies chase them.
Cougars and other wild cats and
coyotes are enemies of raccoons.

Clang! Bang! A noise has waked you up. Raccoons tipped over your trash can, looking for things to eat.

Not many wild animals can live in cities. Raccoons can because they eat so many different things, even garbage! They search for food after dark, when people are indoors. Raccoons can see well at night. Their eyes seem to glow if you shine a light at them.

If you were a raccoon looking for a hiding place
for your den, what would you choose?
Some raccoons make their dens in chimneys.
They can peek outside to see what's going on
or just curl up together inside. Some people put
wire lids on chimneys to keep raccoons out.

With its bushy tail hanging down, a raccoon eats seeds from a bird feeder. Raccoons that live in cities can be little pests. They tip over garbage cans and live in chimneys and eat the food left out for birds.

In a neighborhood where raccoons have become a problem, people set traps for them. Then people called game wardens come and take the raccoons away. Raccoons can be dangerous. Sometimes they have diseases that can make people sick.

Some people leave pet food out for raccoons to eat, but that is not really a good idea. Raccoons are wild animals, not pets. They know how to find food for themselves.

Look carefully at these animals.
Are they raccoons? No.
The animal in the tree is a coati.
It lives in forests in Mexico and
South America. The other animal
lives in parts of our own country.
It is called a ringtail. Can you see why?

Do you see some ways that these
animals look like raccoons?
Scientists say that they
belong to the same family.

Like a little masked robber,
a cub peers out from a hollow log.
The next time you see a raccoon,
you will know a lot about it.

You will know that it is smart and
curious, and that it uses its hands
to explore things. You will know that
it eats many kinds of food and can live
in many different places.
Best of all, you will know that
the raccoon is playful, just like you.

A raccoon cub's shiny black nose and eyes make it look almost like a little stuffed animal. But don't try to cuddle it. Its mother will do that.

COVER: A raccoon family leaves its den at night to look for food.

Published by
The National Geographic Society, Washington, D. C.
Gilbert M. Grosvenor, *President and Chairman of the Board*
Melvin M. Payne, *Chairman Emeritus*
Owen R. Anderson, *Executive Vice President*
Robert L. Breeden, *Senior Vice President,*
 Publications and Educational Media

Prepared by
The Special Publications and School Services Division
Donald J. Crump, *Director*
Philip B. Silcott, *Associate Director*
Bonnie S. Lawrence, *Assistant Director*

Staff for this book
Jane H. Buxton, *Managing Editor*
Charles E. Herron, *Picture Editor*
Lynette R. Ruschak, *Art Director*
Stephen J. Hubbard, *Researcher*
Artemis S. Lampathakis, *Illustrations Assistant*
Sharon K. Berry, Carol R. Curtis, Mary Elizabeth Ellison,
 Rosamund Garner, Bridget A. Johnson, Sandra F. Lotterman,
 Eliza C. Morton, Cleo E. Petroff, Virginia A. Williams,
 Staff Assistants

Engraving, Printing, and Product Manufacture
Robert W. Messer, *Manager*
George V. White, *Assistant Manager*
David V. Showers, *Production Manager*
George J. Zeller, Jr., *Production Project Manager*
Gregory Storer, *Senior Assistant Production Manager*
Mark R. Dunlevy, *Assistant Production Manager*
Timothy H. Ewing, *Production Assistant*

Consultants
Dr. John Hadidian, Urban Wildlife Specialist,
 National Park Service, *Scientific Consultant*
Dr. Ine Noe, *Educational Consultant*
Dr. Lynda Bush, *Reading Consultant*

Illustrations Credits
MASLOWSKI WILDLIFE PRODUCTION (Cover, 18-19); Norman R. Lightfoot (1, 15 lower, 20); Gregory A. Yovan/TOM STACK & ASSOCIATES (2-3, 3); Leonard Lee Rue III (4, 8 lower, 8-9); ANIMALS ANIMALS/C.C. Lockwood (5, 21, 25 lower); C.C. Lockwood (6-7, 13, 24-25); Jen & Des Bartlett/BRUCE COLEMAN INC. (8 upper); Daniel and Julie Cox (10, 11, 15 upper); Martin M. Bruce/SHOSTAL ASSOCIATES (12-13); Millard H. Sharp/BLACK STAR (14-15); Jack Dermid (16 upper, 22); Ted Levin (16 lower); F. Eugene Hester (17); Steve Maslowski/NATIONAL AUDUBON SOCIETY COLLECTION/PR (22-23); C.C. Lockwood/BRUCE COLEMAN INC. (25 upper); C.C. Lockwood/DRK PHOTO (26-27); Marion Patterson/BLACK STAR (27); Tom & Pat Leeson (28, 30-31); Al Nelson/TOM STACK & ASSOCIATES (29); Norman R. Lightfoot/MILLER SERVICES, LTD. (32).

Library of Congress CIP Data
Kostyal, K. M., 1951-
 Raccoons.

 (Books for young explorers)
 Bibliography: p.
 Summary: Introduces the physical characteristics and habits of the raccoon.
 1. Raccoons—Juvenile literature. [1. Raccoons] I. Title. II. Series.
QL737.C26K68   1987   599.74'443   87-5554
ISBN 0-87044-677-0 (regular edition)
ISBN 0-87044-682-7 (library edition)

MORE ABOUT Raccoons

I n the animal world raccoons are a success story. These smart, skillful animals can adapt to living in almost any habitat. Native to North and South America, they are found from desert to seashore, from the countryside to the inner city. Of the seven different raccoon species, five are rare, existing only on islands. The North American, or common, raccoon ranges from Canada to Panama, and the crab-eating raccoon, a semiaquatic species, is found in Central America and parts of South America.

As woodland and wilderness have given way to housing developments and shopping malls, raccoons have learned to take their meals from garbage cans (22-23)* instead of from nut-bearing trees or fish-rich streams. Though they eat both plants and animals, raccoons are classified under the order of carnivores, or meat eaters, because of their tooth structure.

A raccoon has a good memory for where food is located and will return to the same porch day after day if food is left for it (27). But a raccoon's seeming domestication is deceiving. Sooner or later, most "pet" raccoons move on, as they gradually make a shift in the territory, or home range, they patrol.

The size of this home range varies, depending upon the habitat and the age and sex of a given animal. In a city, where every garbage can is a potential food source, a home range may encompass only 11 to 12 acres. In contrast, an animal living in a harsh prairie environment may need to patrol a territory of several thousand acres in order to

*Numbers in parentheses refer to pages in
Raccoons.

TOM & PAT LEESON

Balancing on a log, a raccoon holds a small object in its flexible fingers. The raccoon's coat, dark on the back and lighter underneath, provides camouflage on the ground and in the trees. Gesturing with its bushy tail is one way the animal communicates with other raccoons.

find enough food to survive. Young raccoons tend to range over a larger area than do older animals, and the males usually roam farther than the females.

Within its home range, a raccoon prowls from dusk to dawn, seeking out the spots that are good sources of food and water. As daylight comes on, the animal will find a den to rest in—a hollow in a log or a hole under rocks (30-31). In cold weather, a raccoon chooses a more permanent den, returning to it day after day. A female raccoon with very young cubs also keeps a permanent den, often up in a protected hole in a tree trunk (4).

Like most carnivores, raccoons are born virtually helpless. Averaging about four inches in length and weighing only two ounces, the nearly blind cubs rely completely on their mother. As sole provider for her young, she leaves the nest only briefly to scavenge for food, never venturing far before returning to nurse the cubs (6-7).

Raccoons give birth to litters ranging in size from three to six cubs. When the cubs are about six weeks old, the mother moves them. She carries them one by one in her mouth (8) to another nest that has enough space for them to play together, learning in the process to walk and run and climb. Weaning begins at about this time.

Within several weeks, the cubs are ready to go on short nightly forays with their mother. Soon they are able to stay on the move with her, exploring and feeding at night and finding temporary dens to shelter in during the day. All the while, they are learning by their mother's example how to find food, where dangers lurk, and how, generally, to take care of themselves (8-9). In mild climates, a raccoon litter born

in the spring normally disperses in the fall. In harsher climates, a family will stay together through the winter. In either case, by the time they go off on their own, the young raccoons have learned the lessons of survival from their mother.

The word "raccoon" comes from the name given the animal by the Algonquian Indians: "*Arakun*—he scratches with his hands." Indeed, a raccoon's hands are constantly doing something, whether scratching for insects in a log; finding snails, crayfish, and other small animals in a streambed (18-19); or manipulating some chosen object, seemingly just for the sake of examining it and turning it over.

In recent years, raccoons living in the southeastern United States have suffered from rabies. Scientists are studying ways to control the disease, for the sake of both the animals themselves and the human population and pet animals with which they come in contact.

RACCOONS AND CHILDREN
People and raccoons often live in the same neighborhoods, so it's important for your children to know how to treat these wild animals. What should they do if they see a raccoon near your home?

1. Look: Stand still and watch what the raccoon is doing. Is it looking for food or exploring an empty birdhouse? Observing a creature as it goes about its daily activities is the way scientists learn about animals. You can learn that way, too.

2. Do not touch: Never chase or tease a raccoon or any other wild animal. Trying to catch one could hurt you—and might hurt it as well. Mother raccoons with cubs have been known to attack people who were harassing their young.

3. If you happen to know where a den of newborn raccoons is locat-

ed, remember that the cubs are helpless. You could cause a lot of problems if you disturb them. But if you stand a short distance from the den tree and listen, you might hear them twittering, like baby birds. Occasionally, if a cub is hungry or frightened, it will give a cry that sounds like a human baby's.

4. Check for raccoon tracks in the sand and mud along riverbanks and streambeds (16).

5. If you find a young raccoon alone on the ground, don't pick it up. Its mother probably left it there for a short time and will return for it later. She knows how to care for it far better than you do.

6. Remember that raccoons in the eastern United States may be carriers of rabies and therefore extremely dangerous. Here are some ways you can identify a potentially rabid animal: a) It may be roaming about in full daylight—something healthy raccoons usually don't do. b) It may seem confused or dazed. c) It may walk right into a crowded playground or park.

If you see an animal doing any of these things, walk quickly away and tell a grown-up about it. The grown-up can call the police department or animal shelter to report the animal.

ADDITIONAL READING

A Natural History of Raccoons, by Dorcas MacClintock. (N.Y., Charles Scribner's Sons, 1981). Family reading.

Book of Mammals, 2 vols. (Washington, D. C., National Geographic Society, 1981). Ages 8 and up.

The World of the Raccoon, by Leonard Lee Rue III. (N.Y., J. B. Lippincott Co., 1964). Family reading.